PHYLLIS J. LE

RESOURCES
—FOR—
CARING
PEOPLE

*8 Studies for Groups
or Individuals*

With Notes for Leaders

CARING PEOPLE BIBLE STUDIES

INTERVARSITY PRESS
DOWNERS GROVE, ILLINOIS, USA
LEICESTER, ENGLAND

InterVarsity Press, USA, is the book-publishing division of InterVarsity Christian Fellowship, a student movement active on campus at hundreds of universities, colleges and schools of nursing in the United States of America, and a member movement of the International Fellowship of Evangelical Students. For information about local and regional activities, write Public Relations Dept., InterVarsity Christian Fellowship, 6400 Schroeder Rd., P.O. Box 7895, Madison, WI 53707-7895.

Inter-Varsity Press, UK, is the book-publishing division of the Universities and Colleges Christian Fellowship (formerly the Inter-Varsity Fellowship), a student movement linking Christian Unions in universities and colleges throughout the United Kingdom and the Republic of Ireland, and a member movement of the International Fellowship of Evangelical Students. For information about local and national activities write to UCCF, 38 De Montfort Street, Leicester LE1 7GP.

Some of the studies in this guide are adapted from studies written by Nurses Christian Fellowship staff.

Cover photograph: Michael Goss

USA ISBN 0-8308-1191-5
UK ISBN 0-85111-330-3

Printed in the United States of America

15	14	13	12	11	10	9	8	7	6	5	4	3	2	'
03	02	01	00	99	98	97	96	95	94					

Getting the Most from Caring People Bible Studies

Caring People Bible Studies are designed to show how God equips us to help others who are in need. They reveal what the Bible has to say about the pain we will all face in life and what we can do to care for friends, family, neighbors and even strangers who experience pain.

The passages you will study will be thought-provoking, challenging, inspiring and practical. They will show you how to focus on others, but they will also help you focus on yourself. Why? Because these guides are not designed merely to convince you of the truthfulness of some idea. Rather, they are intended to allow biblical truths to renew your heart and mind.

These Bible studies are inductive rather than deductive. In other words, the author will lead us to discover what the Bible says about a particular topic through a series of questions rather than simply telling us what she believes. Therefore, the studies are thought-provoking. They help us to think about the meaning of the passage so that we can truly understand what the biblical writer intended to say.

Additionally, these studies are personal. At the end of each study, you'll be given an opportunity to make a commitment to respond. And you will find guidance for prayer as well. Finally, these studies are versatile. They are designed for student, professional, neighborhood and/or church groups. They are also effective for individual study.

How They're Put Together
Caring People Bible Studies have a distinctive format. Each study takes about forty-five minutes in a group setting or thirty minutes in personal study—

unless you choose to take more time. The guides have a workbook format with space for writing responses to each question. This is ideal for personal study and allows group members to prepare in advance for the discussion. At the end of the guides are some notes for leaders. They describe how to lead a group discussion, give helpful tips on group dynamics, suggest ways to deal with problems which may arise during the discussion, and provide additional background information on certain questions. With such helps, someone with little or no experience can lead an effective study.

Suggestions for Individual Study

1. As you begin the study, pray that God will help you understand and apply the passages to your life. Pray that he will show you what kinds of action he would have you take as a result of your time of study.

2. In your first session take time to read the introduction to the entire study. This will orient you to the subject at hand and the author's goals for the studies.

3. Read the short introduction to the study.

4. Read and reread the suggested Bible passage to familiarize yourself with it.

5. A good modern translation of the Bible, rather than the King James Version or a paraphrase, will give you the most help. The New International Version, the New American Standard Bible and the Revised Standard Version are all recommended. However, the questions in this guide are based on the New International Version.

6. Use the space provided to respond to the questions. This will help you express your understanding of the passage clearly.

7. It might be good to have a Bible dictionary handy. Use it to look up any unfamiliar words, names or places.

8. Take time with the final question in each study to commit yourself to action and/or a change in attitude.

Suggestions for Group Study

1. Come to the study prepared. Follow the suggestions for individual study mentioned above. You will find that careful preparation will greatly enrich your time spent in group discussion.

2. Be willing to participate in the discussion. The leader of your group will not be lecturing. Instead, he or she will be encouraging the members of the group to discuss what they have learned. The leader will be asking the questions that are found in this guide.

3. Stick to the topic being discussed. Your answers should be based on the verses which are the focus of the discussion and not on outside authorities such as commentaries or speakers.

4. Be sensitive to the other members of the group. Listen attentively when they describe what they have learned. You may be surprised by their insights! When possible, link what you say to the comments of others. Also, be affirming whenever you can. This will encourage some of the more hesitant members of the group to participate.

5. Be careful not to dominate the discussion. We are sometimes so eager to express our thoughts that we leave too little opportunity for others to respond. By all means participate! But allow others to also.

6. Expect God to teach you through the passage being discussed and through the other members of the group. Pray that you will have an enjoyable and profitable time together, but also that as a result of the study, you will find ways that you can take action individually and/or as a group.

7. We recommend that groups follow a few basic guidelines, and that these guidelines be read at the beginning of the first session. The guidelines, which you may wish to adapt to your situation, are:

☐ Anything said in the group is considered confidential and will not be discussed outside the group unless specific permission is given to do so.

☐ We will provide time for each person present to talk if he or she feels comfortable doing so.

☐ We will talk about ourselves and our own situations, avoiding conversation about other people.

☐ We will listen attentively to each other.

☐ We will be very cautious about giving advice.

☐ We will pray for each other.

8. If you are the group leader, you will find additional suggestions at the back of the guide.

Introducing Resources for Caring People

I have written Bible study guides for several years, and I enjoy it very much. A tool that has made the task much easier is the word processor that I am working on right now. The more my knowledge and awareness of how to use this computer grows, the greater my ease in writing. There are still many resources within the computer that are of no value to me because I don't know they are there or I don't know how to use them.

Caring for others is much the same. God not only calls us to be caring people but also equips us with resources—many valuable resources. That is what this study guide is all about.

This guide is for those who desire to be obedient to God in caring for others. It is to help us to be aware of the resources that God has given us and to find out how to more fully develop these resources for his glory.

There are eight resources discussed in this guide: Scripture, prayer, God's Spirit, past experiences, healthy self-image, listening, obedience and the Christian community.

Some of these resources, such as Scripture, prayer and the Holy Spirit are the more obvious resources which are available to every Christian. They are vital in carrying out the task of caring for others. Looking at what the Bible teaches about prayer, seeing the work of the Holy Spirit in Romans, and looking at what Scripture can offer in Psalms, helps us to be more aware of these resources in our lives and motivates us to use them more freely.

We may be uncertain about the availability of the other resources. Maybe you are not convinced that "just" listening to another is really helpful. Or that when you share the pain from your past another person is touched. In some instances you don't even share a word about that pain but your attitude toward a hurting person has been softened because of it. Healing occurs when someone takes another person seriously and listens actively.

To better understand these dynamics, we will look at the difference listening to God and listening to others makes. Additionally, we will see how our experiences of being comforted by God enable us to comfort others.

As you look over the list of resources, you might ask how obedience affects your ability to care for others. Or wonder, "What if my self-image isn't healthy?" You might realize that you don't even know what Christian community is all about and wonder how it can be a resource for caring. As you work through these studies, may these resources become more clear to you as new understanding is ingrained into your heart.

Just as it is my goal to learn more about the resources available to me through my computer, it is my prayer for you and me that we will become more aware of the resources that God has given to us. And I pray that we will strive to use and develop these gifts as we care for others.

1/Past Experiences
2 Corinthians 1:1-11

I will never forget the note that was waiting for my husband, Andy, when we arrived home from Minnesota. Andy had just watched his mother die very unexpectedly. (He'd lost his dad seven years earlier.) The note was from a friend who had also lost both parents. She wrote that losing a second parent always seemed harder than losing the first because without either parent you were an orphan. Someone else had been through his experience and was willing to share what it was like. Someone else knew what he was feeling. That brought Andy comfort.

When we experience pain, we can comfort people who are hit with a similar loss. Similarly, Paul was grateful for the opportunity to experience God's comfort, so that he in turn could comfort others.

1. How do you respond when someone says you will be able to help others because of what you are going through?

2. Read 2 Corinthians 1:1-11. Why is Paul so full of praise to God?

3. According to Paul, how do our troubles and sufferings serve a worthwhile purpose?

_____

4. What has suffering taught Paul about God?

_____

5. How can each of these characteristics of God that Paul learned about through suffering help you in times of trouble?

_____

6. Recall a specific time when you experienced trouble or suffering. What did you learn about yourself, others or God?

_____

7. How have you been able to help others because you went through that experience?

8. We need to experience healing in order to bring God's healing to others. In what areas of your life do you need God to heal you?

9. After talking about suffering in general earlier in the chapter, why do you think Paul goes into much greater detail about what he suffered in Asia (vv. 8-11)?

10. How was Paul helped by those he had helped (v. 11)?

11. When have you been helped by someone who has experienced suffering in his or her past?

12. How do you feel more ready to help others because of what you see in this passage?

Ask God to help you show others the comfort that you have received from him. Thank God for the comfort and deliverance he has provided to you in the past.

2/Healthy Self-Image
John 13:1-17

L ynn was weeping. She was sharing how she had misjudged a friend's motives. She thought Georgia had accused her of not being capable of leading the meeting the next day. Actually, Georgia was genuinely concerned about the signs of burnout she had seen in Lynn and wanted to offer help. Lynn went on to say, "I suspected Georgia of thinking I was not capable because that's the way I feel about myself."

Self-esteem (feelings about self) and self-concept (knowledge about self) make up our self-image. The way I *think* about myself has a tremendous effect on the way I *feel* about myself and respond to others. It is exciting to look at Jesus and see how clearly he knew who he was. Because of this, he felt sure of himself and was able to focus on others—even when he was facing death.

---

1. What does it mean to accept yourself?

2. Read John 13:1-17. What did Jesus know about himself (vv. 1-3)?

What was the significance of that knowledge?

3. Jesus' knowledge about himself was directly tied to his secure relationship with God. How does your knowledge about yourself compare and contrast with that of Jesus? (Consider his sense of timing, his sense of purpose, and his relationship with God.)

4. Does what you know about yourself (self-concept) always correlate with how you feel about yourself (self-esteem)? Why or why not?

5. How was Jesus able to care for others as a result of knowing who he was (vv. 4-5, 13-14, 16)?

6. Foot-washing, a sign of hospitality, was usually performed by a slave. What would be a similar way for you to care for someone in need?

7. Besides performing the menial task of foot-washing, Jesus was able to accept the disciples as they were. What evidence is there of this throughout the passage?

Why is accepting people vital in order to be able to care for them?

8. Jesus said, "You call me 'Teacher and Lord,' and rightly so, for that is what I am." How should your self-image be affected by the fact that you are related to Jesus and are his student and subject?

9. As a follower of Jesus, in what ways do you need to grow toward a healthier self-image?

How can you do this?

10. How can we help others grow toward a healthier self-image?

11. Jesus knew who he was. He served and accepted others freely. How does your self-image and knowing who you are in Christ affect the way you are able to care for others?

Pray for a healthier self-image that will make it possible to give to others. Ask God to reveal various ways you can serve others.

3/Listening
Isaiah 50:4-5; 42:1-4

I n A View from a Hearse *Joe Bayly wrote of his feelings while at the wake* of his young son. One friend, he said, sat down by him and talked from the time he came until the time he left. Joe was glad to see that person go. Another friend sat by his side in silence, occasionally asking a question. He was sad when that person went, but he had been comforted.

1. Would you describe yourself as more a listener or a talker? Why?

2. Read Isaiah 50:4-5. This passage, sometimes called a "Servant Song," is a prophetic description of Jesus, who is the speaker. According to these verses, what has the Sovereign Lord done to and for Jesus?

LISTENING 19

3. What do you think it means "to have an instructed tongue" and "to know the word that sustains the weary"?

4. What does it mean to "listen like one being taught" and to open your ears?

5. How do you think listening to God is related to knowing how to listen and respond to people in need?

6. Think of a time when you were weary and someone said just the right thing. What was it like?

7. Describe a time when shortcuts were taken and someone tried to say the right thing to you without long and hard listening.

8. Read Isaiah 42:1-4. This passage is the first "Servant Song." How is Jesus' gentleness demonstrated in verses 2-3?

9. As disciples of Jesus, we want his character to be built in us. How is gentleness an important ingredient in being an effective listener?

10. Often when people are hurting, it is over an injustice. What hope does this passage offer to such a person?

11. How might we "break a bruised reed" or "snuff out a smoldering wick" by the way we listen?

12. Why is faithfulness to the person speaking vital when listening to someone?

13. Think of a person in your life who needs to be listened to. What can you do this week to begin to meet that need?

Pray for that person. Ask God to meet this person through you.

4/Obedience
Luke 22:39-53

Following God is not an easy task. Many times it will mean taking the difficult road. It can also lead to pain and suffering. However, obeying God will *always* lead to a great sense of peace and contentment. It is important not to oversimplify the process of accepting God's will for us. In this passage we see how Jesus struggled to accept the task his Father had for him.

1. When have you had difficulty accepting God's will for your life? Why?

2. Read Luke 22:39-53. How do you see Jesus dealing with the agony of facing the cross (vv. 39-42)?

3. What evidence is there that Jesus' statement "Yet not my will, but yours be done" was acceptance, not passive resignation (vv. 43-44)?

4. Throughout the passage, what signs do you see of Christ's deep sorrow?

What signs do you see of the disciples' deep sorrow (v. 45)?

5. When might your caring for another cause you sorrow?

6. What further evidence is there in verses 47-53 that Jesus meant it when he said, "Your will be done"?

7. What about how Jesus dealt with accepting the cross might help you to obey God especially in the area of caring for others?

8. In what ways have you experienced the deep peace and the deep sorrow that can come with accepting difficult and painful tasks?

9. How were others affected by Jesus' obedience? (Consider the disciples, the crowd, Judas, and the servant of the high priest who had his ear cut off.)

10. How are you affected by those who are able to truly obey God?

11. How is willingness to obey God a resource when caring for someone in need?

Pray that God will increase your understanding of himself and his will for you—and that you'll grow in your acceptance of his will.

5/Scripture
Psalm 19

I remember when Joy asked, "How do I get to know God?" We looked at the story of Nicodemus in John's Gospel and discussed being born into God's family. Eventually, Joy became a Christian. Then there was Tom who was frightened before going to surgery. I shared thoughts with him from Psalm 23 about our Shepherd who gives us all we need and goes with us through dark valleys. Tom didn't have to be afraid because Jesus was with him. He seemed to be at peace.

Sharing Scripture may not always be the right thing to help someone, but often it is. Psalm 19 describes what Scripture is like and how it can help.

1. How does God most clearly communicate with you?

2. Read Psalm 19. What does creation reveal about God (vv. 1-6)?

3. What have you learned about God through your observations and enjoyment of nature?

4. If you did not have the Bible and could only learn about God through nature, what information would you be lacking about him?

5. The terms *law, statutes, precepts, commands* and *ordinances* in this passage are synonyms for Scripture. In verses 7-11, how are the Scriptures described?

What do they do?

6. From which of these effects of Scripture have you benefited? Explain.

7. How might these effects of Scripture benefit those you are trying to care for?

8. What is the overall effect of the psalmist's encounter with God through nature and the Scriptures (vv. 12-14)?

9. How has this psalm been helpful to you as you consider how important Scripture is to someone in need?

10. Sharing Scripture can be done in three ways. The first and most obvious way is sharing a passage or verse directly. The second is sharing how we have been affected or changed by Scripture. The third is simply living out the principles of Scripture. How might you appropriately and effectively share Scripture with someone in need this week?

Ask God to make Scripture alive and active in you this week. Pray that he will help you share his Word, either directly or through actions, with someone in need.

6/Prayer
Luke 11:1-13

Upperclassmen prayed for each of us by name before we arrived at the school of nursing as freshmen. As a result those of us who were Christians when we came felt supported and loved, and we grew in the Lord. Many who did not know Jesus when they arrived left three years later as maturing Christians. The theme throughout the dormitory became Hudson Taylor's, "Man is moved by God through prayer alone."

1. What is a good father like?

2. Read Luke 11:1-13. What causes the disciples to ask Jesus to teach them to pray (v. 1)?

3. What is the significance of Jesus telling the disciples to address God as *Father*?

4. How does your relationship with God compare with your relationship with your parents?

5. Why can God be trusted more than earthly parents (vv. 11-13)?

6. Think about each petition of Jesus' prayer. What would it mean to you if God granted each one of them?

7. How is each of Jesus' requests a priority of life and therefore central to what we should pray for?

8. According to verse 8, what causes the man to give his friend the bread?

9. What does it mean for us to approach God boldly?

10. Sometimes a way to care for someone is to let them help you. What usually causes you to hesitate to ask a friend for help?

11. What is implied about your relationship with a person when you do ask him or her for help?

12. How is our relationship with God like a friendship?

In what ways does it surpass friendship?

13. Jesus promises, "Ask and it will be given to you; seek and you will find; knock and the door will be opened to you" (v. 9). How do you respond to these promises as you think about praying for yourself and for others?

Ask God to help you to be a good steward of the resource of prayer.

7/God's Spirit

Romans 8:1-27

I have a strong desire to help people. But my strong desire to help becomes a weakness if I'm not waiting on the Spirit of God to lead and to work in people. Sometimes I try to fix things myself. And I want people fixed now. God wants people helped too, but his work is not on my timetable.

The book of Romans has helped me to understand more about the working of the Holy Spirit. In this passage we learn more about how to make the Holy Spirit's life our own.

1. Describe a time when you felt a need for the Holy Spirit's work in your life.

2. Read Romans 8:1-27. Verses 1-4 declare the good news that we have been set free from sin and death by God's Spirit through Christ Jesus. How does

Paul contrast this life in the Spirit with life in the sinful nature (vv. 5-11)?

3. According to verses 12-17, in what ways does the Holy Spirit become involved in our lives?

4. How have you experienced the Spirit's involvement in your life in those ways?

5. Why is suffering still present in the lives of Christians (vv. 17-23)?

6. What do you think it means to share in Christ's sufferings?

7. According to this passage, what is the meaning of *hope* (vv. 24-25)?

8. How does hope affect our ability to endure suffering?

9. Describe how God's Spirit helps us in our weakness (vv. 26-27).

10. What potential suffering do you fear?

11. What difference does it make to you that God's Spirit would be living in you, praying for you and giving you hope during such a crisis?

12. What evidence does Paul give to show God cares about you?

How can you relate this to someone who is suffering and who might question God's concern?

13. How is God's Spirit a resource to you as you care for someone who is suffering?

Ask the Holy Spirit to be a resource in your life and to help you in your weakness as you seek to care for others.

8/Christian Community
Acts 4:23-37

Next to the Vietnam Memorial in Washington, D.C., stands a statue of three men: a Black, a Hispanic and a White soldier. They are standing very close together. The tour guide, a soldier who fought in Nam, explained the significance of the statue. He said more minorities from our country fought in Vietnam than had ever before. And they were standing so close together because in Vietnam they learned, like never before, how very much they needed each other.

In Acts 4 the religious leaders were greatly disturbed because Peter and John were teaching the people and proclaiming Jesus' resurrection. Something had to be done! Peter and John were arrested, jailed overnight, brought before the Sanhedrin, threatened and then let go. The first place they went was back to "their people," the Christian community.

1. When have you been supported by a group?

2. Read Acts 4:23-37. Imagine that you were in the group of believers to whom John and Peter returned. What would have been your reaction?

---

3. What was the reaction of the believers (vv. 23-30)?

---

4. The *New English Bible* translation of verse 24 is "they raised their voices as one man and called upon God." What do you think were the physical, emotional and spiritual benefits of such unity in this community of believers?

---

5. When have you experienced the benefits of this kind of unity in your community?

---

6. The believers addressed God as *Sovereign Lord* (v. 24). How would you define *sovereign*?

7. What does their prayer reveal about their faith in the character of God?

8. Two-thirds of their prayer focused on God's character, faithfulness and acts in the past. What did they finally request of God in the last part of their prayer (vv. 29-30)?

9. What would you have asked of God in the same situation?

10. When they asked for boldness, God answered mightily. The meeting place shook, they were filled with the Holy Spirit, and they spoke the Word of God openly and with confidence. What was the community like after this (vv. 32-37)?

11. Verse 34 says, "There were no needy persons among them." How is your Christian community similar to the one in Acts, and how is it different?

12. How is Christian community a resource for your own spiritual well-being?

13. How can you provide support and Christian community to someone in your life who is in need?

Ask God to give you renewed appreciation for the Christian community he has given you. Pray that he will use you to provide community for someone in need.

Leader's Notes

Leading a Bible discussion can be an enjoyable and rewarding experience. But it can also be intimidating—especially if you've never done it before. If this is how you feel, you're in good company.

When God asked Moses to lead the Israelites out of Egypt, he replied, "O Lord, please send someone else to do it!" (Ex 4:13). But God's response to all of his servants—including you—is essentially the same: "My grace is sufficient for you" (2 Cor 12:9).

There is another reason you should feel encouraged. Leading a Bible discussion is not difficult if you follow certain guidelines. You don't need to be an expert on the Bible or a trained teacher. The suggestions listed below should enable you to effectively and enjoyably fulfill your role as leader.

Using Caring People Bible Studies

Where should you begin? A good starting place is *Handbook for Caring People*. This short book helps develop some basic caring skills like listening to and communicating to people who are in pain. Additionally, it will help you understand the stages that people in grief go through and how to help people who are suffering. Most of all, this book shows how to rely on God for the strength you need to care for others. At the end of each chapter, you'll find questions for individual or group use.

For the next step you might choose *Resources for Caring People* or *The*

Character of Caring People. *Resources for Caring People* will show how God empowers us to serve others through Scripture, prayer, the Holy Spirit and many other gifts. *The Character of Caring People* shows what the heart of the Christian caregiver is like. The concerns which emerge within the group during the studies will provide you with guidance for what to do next. All of the guides give help and encouragement to those who want to care for others, but different groups may find some guides more useful than others.

You might want to focus on specific concerns like *Caring for People in Grief* or *Caring for People in Conflict*. Or your group might choose to study topics which reflect areas they need to grow in. For instance, those who have sick friends or relatives or who simply want to be more sensitive to the physical needs that are all around us will find *Caring for Physical Needs* helpful. Others may want to know more about the spiritual concerns people have. *Caring for Spiritual Needs* is a great resource for this. For a biblical perspective on how God wants us to deal with emotional problems, you might choose *Caring for Emotional Needs*. The key is to remember that we all have these needs. Our physical condition affects us spiritually and emotionally. A spiritual problem can have physical and emotional consequences. By covering several of these guides in sequence, members of your group will develop a complete picture of what it means to be a caring Christian.

Preparing for the Study

1. Ask God to help you understand and apply the passage in your own life. Unless this happens, you will not be prepared to lead others. Pray too for the various members of the group. Ask God to open your hearts to the message of his Word and to motivate you to action.

2. Read the introduction to the entire guide to get an overview of the subject at hand and the issues which will be explored.

3. As you begin each study, read and reread the assigned Bible passage to familiarize yourself with it.

4. This study guide is based on the New International Version of the Bible. It will help you and the group if you use this translation as the basis for your study and discussion.

5. Carefully work through each question in the study. Spend time in meditation and reflection as you consider how to respond.

6. Write your thoughts and responses in the space provided in the study guide. This will help you to express your understanding of the passage clearly.

7. It might help you to have a Bible dictionary handy. Use it to look up any unfamiliar words, names or places. (For additional help on how to study a passage, see chapter five of *Leading Bible Discussions*, IVP.)

8. Take the response portion of each study seriously. Consider what this means for your life—what changes you might need to make in your lifestyle and/or actions you need to take in the world. Remember that the group will follow your lead in responding to the studies.

Leading the Study

1. Begin the study on time. Open with prayer, asking God to help the group to understand and apply the passage.

2. Be sure that everyone in your group has a study guide. Encourage the group to prepare beforehand for each discussion by reading the introduction to the guide and by working through the questions in the study.

3. At the beginning of your first time together, explain that these studies are meant to be discussions, not lectures. Encourage the members of the group to participate. However, do not put pressure on those who may be hesitant to speak during the first few sessions.

4. Have a group member read the introductory paragraph at the beginning of the discussion. This will orient the group to the topic of the study.

5. Every study begins with an "approach" question, which is meant to be asked before the passage is read. These questions are important for several reasons.

First, there is always a stiffness that needs to be overcome before people will begin to talk openly. A good question will break the ice.

Second, most people will have lots of different things going on in their minds (dinner, an important meeting coming up, how to get the car fixed) that will have nothing to do with the study. A creative question will get their attention and draw them into the discussion.

Third, approach questions can reveal where our thoughts or feelings need to be transformed by Scripture. That is why it is especially important not to read the passage before the approach question is asked. The passage will tend to color the honest reactions people would otherwise give because they are, of course, supposed to think the way the Bible does.

6. Have a group member read aloud the passage to be studied.

7. As you ask the questions, keep in mind that they are designed to be used just as they are written. You may simply read them aloud. Or you may prefer to express them in your own words. There may be times when it is appropriate to deviate from the study guide. For example, a question may have already been answered. If so, move on to the next question. Or someone may raise an important question not covered in the guide. Take time to discuss it, but try to keep the group from going off on tangents.

8. Avoid answering your own questions. If necessary, repeat or rephrase them until they are clearly understood. An eager group quickly becomes passive and silent if they think the leader will do most of the talking.

9. Don't be afraid of silence. People may need time to think about the question before formulating their answers.

10. Don't be content with just one answer. Ask, "What do the rest of you think?" or "Anything else?" until several people have given answers to the question.

11. Acknowledge all contributions. Try to be affirming whenever possible. Never reject an answer. If it is clearly off-base, ask, "Which verse led you to that conclusion?" or again, "What do the rest of you think?"

12. Don't expect every answer to be addressed to you, even though this will probably happen at first. As group members become more at ease, they will begin to truly interact with each other. This is one sign of healthy discussion.

13. Don't be afraid of controversy. It can be very stimulating. If you don't resolve an issue completely, don't be frustrated. Move on and keep it in mind for later. A subsequent study may solve the problem.

14. Periodically summarize what the group has said about the passage. This helps to draw together the various ideas mentioned and gives continuity to the study. But don't preach.

15. Don't skip over the response questions. It's important that we not lose the focus of helping others even as we reflect on ourselves. Be willing to get things started by describing how you have been affected by the study.

16. Conclude your time together with conversational prayer. Ask for God's help in following through on the commitments you've made.

17. End on time. Many more suggestions and helps are found in *Small Group Leader's Handbook* and *Good Things Come in Small Groups* (both from IVP). Reading through one of these books would be worth your time.

Listening to Emotional Pain

Caring People Bible Studies are designed to take seriously the pain and struggle that is part of life. People will experience a variety of emotions during these studies. Keep in mind that you are not expected to act as a professional counselor. However, part of your role as group leader may be to listen to emotional pain. Listening is a gift which you can give to a person who is hurting. For many people, it is not an easy gift to give. The following suggestions will help you to listen more effectively to people in emotional pain.

1. Remember that you are not responsible to take the pain away. People in helping relationships often feel that they are being asked to make the other person feel better. This may be related to the helper not being comfortable with painful feelings.

2. Not only are you not responsible to take the pain away, one of the things people need most is an opportunity to face and to experience the pain in their lives. Many have spent years denying their pain and running from it. Healing can come when we are able to face our pain in the presence of someone who cares about us. Rather than trying to take the pain away, then, commit yourself to listening attentively as it is expressed.

3. Realize that some group members may not feel comfortable with others' expressions of sadness or anger. You may want to acknowledge that such emotions are uncomfortable, but say that learning to feel our own pain is often the first step in helping others with their pain.

4. Be very cautious about giving answers and advice. Advice and answers may make you feel better or feel competent, but they may also minimize people's problems and their painful feelings. Simple solutions rarely work, and they can easily communicate "You should be better now" or "You shouldn't really be talking about this."

5. Be sure to communicate direct affirmation any time people talk about their painful emotions. It takes courage to talk about our pain because it creates anxiety for us. It is a great gift to be trusted by those who are struggling.

The following notes refer to specific questions in the study:

Study 1. Past Experiences. 2 Corinthians 1:1-11.

Purpose: To see how the comfort we have received from God in the past can be used to comfort others.

Question 2. The purpose of this question is to scan the whole passage and get a feel for what Paul is talking about when he speaks of the need for comfort and where it comes from. Do not linger on it too long.

Question 4. Start with verse 1 and consider all that Paul says about God.

Question 8. Group members may want to respond in general terms to this question, or they may relate specific experiences of pain. Be ready to listen to and encourage individuals as they share.

Question 9. It is not until we get to this paragraph that we get a real sense of the extreme suffering Paul had been through. This should make us appreciate all the more his thoughts on the value of his suffering and how he had been comforted by God. The depth of his suffering adds credibility to his comments.

Study 2. Healthy Self-Image. John 13:1-17.

Purpose: To see how a healthy self-image is a resource of a caring person and how our relationship with Jesus can affect our self-image.

General Note: It should be noted that some of the application in this study comes from a secondary interpretation of the passage. The primary thrust of this passage is to teach us to be servants because Jesus our Lord and Savior is a servant. The writer is going from the greater to the lesser in arguing his point: "Now that I, your Lord and Teacher, have washed your feet, you also should wash one another's feet." In other words, if Jesus, who is far greater than we are, was willing to do menial service, how much more should we, who are merely his servants?

However, there is room for considering the fact that Jesus clearly knew who he was and that this affected how he responded to others. Certainly our relationship with God is the very core of a healthy self-image. And though we serve others out of obedience to our Lord and by following his example, our self-image affects the way we are able to do this.

Question 2-3. This is a vital question in the study and should not be passed over lightly. Help the group to discuss each aspect of Jesus' knowledge: (1) God's timing in his life. He knew that it was time to go to the Father: "Jesus knew that the time had come for him to leave this world and go to the Father." (2) He has a sense of purpose. He loved those in the world who belonged to him: "Having loved his own who were in the world, he now showed them the full extent of his love." (3) Jesus knew where he had come from, his purpose and destination: "he had come from God and was returning to God." He was confident about his relationship with God. He knew God was in control and had not left him: "Jesus knew that the Father had put all things under his power."

Question 4. If truth about ourselves always fit together with how we feel about ourselves, we would be in good shape most of the time. At least we would have an accurate self-image. Unfortunately, this is usually not the case. Many things affect the way we feel about ourselves—not just what we know to be true. A few of these are: how others respond to us, the degree of our physical health, how rested we are, and the circumstances we are currently facing.

Question 5. Be sure to note the introductory remarks written after the purpose of this study above.

Question 6. The washing of the disciples' feet was an act of servanthood and humility. Only servants washed feet. Being servants in this day and age is not a popular concept. It is important to think through ways to serve others by identifying what would be equivalent to foot-washing today: mopping someone's floor, grocery shopping, cleaning bathrooms, listening to someone who is difficult to listen to, and so on.

Question 7. Jesus gave a serious response to Peter's questions. He acknowledged and accepted the fact that Peter did not understand now what Jesus was doing. He also communicated acceptance to Judas by washing his feet, though he knew Judas was going to betray him.

Question 10. There are all sorts of ways that members of the body of Christ can communicate value, worth and affirmation to other members of the body.

Explore possible ways of doing this.

Study 3. Listening. Isaiah 50:4-5; 42:1-4.
Purpose: To be motivated to become better listeners to God and to others.
Question 2. There is more than one possibility for the identity of the servant in this passage. *The New Bible Dictionary: Revised* under "servant" states: "1. there is a collective view in which the servant seems to be Israel, 2. an individual view which sometimes sees the servant as the prophet himself, but most often as the messiah and 3. an individual/collective view which sees the messiah as representative of Israel." Whatever view is taken, the passage certainly finds its ultimate fulfillment in Jesus the Messiah.
Question 4. *The NIV Study Bible* states in reference to verse 4 that "unlike Israel (see v. 2), the servant was responsive to God." Likewise *opened my ears* is intrepreted as "a sign of obedience (see 1:19; Ps. 40:6)" in contrast to rebelliousness. The Messiah is listening to and being obedient to the Lord.
Question 5. Showing love by really listening to others in need takes energy and wisdom. God is the source of the energy and wisdom we need. Our world is preoccupied with action, activity and quick fixes. As in other areas of our Christian life and ministry, we often try to take shortcuts and move out on our own instead of being quiet before God and listening to him first and foremost before listening to others. All too often, then, we give quick and impatient answers without listening long and hard to the person who is hurting.
Questions 6-7. It will be crucial for you as the leader to have good examples to illustrate the principles of listening. This will spark memories of relevant experiences in group members and encourages them to talk. In this type of question the group leader may want to answer first.
Question 8. It should be noted that some of the application of Isaiah 42:1-4 comes from a secondary interpretation of the passage. The primary theme of the passage concerns Jesus bringing justice to the nations (vv. 1, 3-4). However, the character of Jesus that is spoken of is clearly a vital part of being effective and godly listeners. These characteristics are what we are looking at closely in the second half of this study.
Question 12. Think about the kind of faithfulness you want when someone

is listening to you—faithfulness in keeping confidence, continuing to listen, and loving you no matter what you say.

Study 4. Obedience. Luke 22:39-53.

Purpose: To see how Jesus faced, accepted and chose to obey in the very difficult situation of going to the cross.

Question 2. There is much to take into consideration in these four short verses. Jesus dealt with the cross as he did with all of life—he prayed. He "went out *as usual* to the Mount of Olives." The fact that Judas knew where to reach him also indicates that Jesus visited his place of prayer regularly. He not only prayed but instructed his disciples to pray. He was well aware of the temptations that faced them all. He took his disciples with him for community and support as well as for their instruction. He honestly presented his need and desire to the Father and asked him to do something about it. It was after all of this that he said, "Not my will but yours be done."

Question 6. Look at Jesus' response to Judas, to the disciple's suggestion that they strike with their swords, to the servant who had his ear cut off and at Jesus' statement: "But this is your hour when darkness reigns."

Question 8. Let there be times of silence as group members think about how to respond. Struggling to accept situations can be very painful and difficult to share. Be ready as a leader to describe your personal experiences.

Question 9. This question leaves room for speculation. How would members of your group have felt if they had been these individuals or a member of the crowd? How would they have been affected?

The disciples that Jesus found sleeping were confronted by him but probably felt accepted and loved in spite of their failure to "watch and pray." Jesus knew they were "exhausted from sorrow." They were given another chance. They also had a vivid lesson on the importance of prayer. They saw Jesus turn to the Father in his most agonizing hour. They were also instructed by him to pray so that they would not fall into temptation.

Think through all that the crowd observed and how they would have been affected. How was Judas received by Jesus? What would have been a normal human response to being betrayed? How would the servant of the high priest have been affected by being healed by the person he was taking captive?

Study 5. Scripture. Psalm 19.

Purpose: To consider the impact of Scripture on our own lives and on the lives of those we are caring for.

Question 2. According to *The New Bible Commentary:*

The wonder of the sky is a constant stimulus to praise in the book of Psalms. The emphasis here is upon objective testimony rather than subjective interpretations. 1 The heavens ceaselessly declare the glory of God; *the firmament,* or extended expanse of the sky, reveals Him by being His workmanship; 2 each day speaks to the following day and each night makes Him known. 3, 4 While they themselves are silent and inarticulate, their testimony is heard everywhere.

Far from worshipping the sun, the psalmist regards it as an agent of God who has set up a tent in the vast heavens for the sun's use. Certainly the wide range of the sun's light and heat is a reflection of God's universal power and knowledge. This thought leads to a meditation upon the inward light afforded by the law or Torah. (*The New Bible Commentary,* p. 462.)

Question 6. Help the group to move from a theoretical observation of what Scripture did for the psalmist to thinking through and sharing what those affects have meant to them. For example, when have their souls been revived, or when have they been given wisdom for a specific situation, or given joy as a result of having been in Scripture? Again, if Scripture is not alive and bringing about change in our lives, it will be difficult for us to share it in such a way that it will be used in the lives of people around us in need.

Question 7. It should not be difficult to move to this question if there has been a realization of how we have been helped by Scripture (see question 6).

Question 10. There are three ways of "sharing Scripture." The first and most obvious is to overtly share a particular passage that seems to be appropriate and significant for a certain need. The second is to verbalize how we have been affected or changed by Scripture. The other way is to share my life in a way that is helpful to someone in need. This is possible because I have been affected or changed by Scripture. Sometimes "living out" Scripture is the only way to share it effectively with those who don't believe it.

Study 6. Prayer. Luke 11:1-13.

Purpose: To examine how Jesus taught his disciples to pray and to consider how prayer is a resource of the caring person.

Question 2. It is significant that it was after Jesus had prayed that his disciples asked him to teach them to pray. They wanted to learn what he was modeling and what they knew to be important to him. The other cause is the more obvious: "Just as John taught his disciples."

Question 3. Be sure to take time to think through as many of the character-istics and responsibilities of a good father and therefore the implications of calling God "Father." What is a good father like? What does he do? What are his responsibilities? I emphasize *good* father because not everyone in the group will have necessarily experienced good fathering. A person's view of and relationship with God is tremendously affected by his relationship with his earthly father.

"Father is the translation of the Aramaic *Abba* used by Jesus (cf. 10:21; Mk. 14:36); here, therefore, Jesus introduces His disciples to the same intimate relationship with the Father which He enjoyed" (*The New Bible Commentary,* p. 906).

Question 4. Be sensitive to the fact that there will be those in your group who may not have experienced good fathering or good parenting. There may be a need to discuss how to overcome the wounds from such a relationship in order to be able to relate to God as Father.

Question 6-7. Do not allow these questions to be passed over quickly. Con-sider each request in as much depth as is possible. This is the pivotal question of the study because the content of what Jesus taught the disciples to pray should guide us in the way we pray.

Hallowed be thy name is the first of two petitions concerned with God Himself. May His name, which represents His Person, be honoured and accepted in the world of men. Such hallowing forms the basis for the second petition: *Thy kingdom come.* May God's rule in peace and righteous-ness swiftly come about. It is a prayer for God to act by hastening the coming of the day of the Lord. Only after these petitions are the needs of the petitioner mentioned.

First, there is a prayer for the supply of *daily bread each day.* Commentators increasingly see here a petition not simply for ordinary food (though this is included) but for the bread of life, the gift of God without which man cannot live. Second, there is a prayer for daily forgiveness, which is granted only to those who forgive others. Finally, the petitioner asks to be preserved from tribulation and testing which would weaken his faith and exclude him from God's kingdom. (*The New Bible Commentary*, p. 906.)

Study 7. God's Spirit. Romans 8:1-27.

Purpose: To examine the results of God's Spirit being active in my own life and how he can help me to care for others.

Question 4. This is the opportunity to go from the theoretical to the practical. It is one thing to talk about how Scripture says God should become involved in our lives and another to share how this has actually happened.

Question 5. This passage throws great light on one basic reason for suffering: we are in a fallen world, and we groan for the redemptive process to be completed. But there are other reasons too. It is our privilege as Christians to share in Christ's sufferings. Because of this, we will also share in his glory. Not only does that give hope for the future, but having suffered increases our appreciation for his glory: "I consider that our present sufferings are not worth comparing with the glory that will be revealed in us" (Rom 8:18).

Question 6. The purpose of this question is to have the group discuss, first, what it means to share in Christ's suffering and, second, what the practical implications are of doing so. The discussion should center on the theme of being a caring person.

Paul may be quoting a familiar saying of the early church (cf. 2 Timothy 2:11-13) that believers experiencing adoption are co-heirs with Christ if indeed "they share His sufferings that they may share His glory too." The Christian's life is a reproduction of the life of Christ. *We suffer with him* implies the communion of cross-bearing or self-sacrifice; not that our experiences are redemptive in themselves, but we "complete what is lacking in Christ's afflictions" (see Colossians 1:24). (*The New Bible Commentary*, p. 1031.)

Question 10. This discussion should be handled with care. It can be difficult to share the fears we have about suffering. The more vulnerable the group, the more helpful the study.

Study 8. Christian Community. Acts 4:23-37.

Purpose: To realize the importance of the Christian community as a resource for helping those in need.

Question 4. After the difficult experiences they had been through, there was probably a deep sense of joy from just being with the people from their Christian community. Then to be so unified that they called on God "as one man" not only meant power in prayer but also a deep sense of emotional satisfaction and well-being.

Question 6. Here are a couple possible definitions: "*Sovereign Lord,* . . . The opening words of this prayer probably illustrate early Christian liturgical practice, based on Jewish liturgical forms. The phraseology of the exordium echoes such O.T. passages as Ex. 20:11, Ne. 9:6, Ps. 146:6" (*The New Bible Commentary,* pp. 977-78).

"Sovereign: 1. above or superior to all others; chief, greatest, supreme. 2. supreme in power, rank or authority. 3. of or holding the position of ruler; royal; reigning. 4. independent of all others" (*Webster's New World Dictionary of the American Language*).

About the Author

Phyllis J. Le Peau is a registered nurse and a former Nurses Christian Fellowship staffworker. Currently, she is assistant program director for Wellness, Inc. Phyllis is also the author of the Fruit of the Spirit Bible Studies Kindness, Gentleness and Joy (Zondervan) and coauthor of Disciplemakers' Handbook (IVP). With her husband, Andy, she has coauthored One Plus One Equals One and the LifeGuide® Bible Studies Ephesians and James (IVP/SU). She and her husband live in Downers Grove, Illinois, with their four children.

Caring People Bible Studies from InterVarsity Press
By Phyllis J. Le Peau

Handbook for Caring People (coauthored by Bonnie J. Miller). This book provides simple, time-tested principles for dealing with the pain, the questions and the crises people face. You will get the basic tools for communication plus some practical suggestions. Questions for group discussion are at the end of each chapter.

Resources for Caring People. Through God, we have the resources we need to help others. God has given us Scripture, prayer, the Holy Spirit, listening and acceptance. This guide will show you how he works through people like you every day. 8 studies.

The Character of Caring People. The key to caring is character. These Bible studies will show you how to focus on the gifts of caring which God has given you—such as hospitality, generosity and encouragement. 8 studies.

Caring for Spiritual Needs. A relationship with God. Meaning and purpose. Belonging. Love. Assurance. These are just some of the spiritual needs that we all have. This Bible study guide will help you learn how these needs can be met in your life and in the lives of others. 9 studies.

Caring for Emotional Needs. We think we have to act like we have it all together, yet sometimes we are lonely, afraid or depressed. Christians have emotional needs just like everyone else. This Bible study guide shows how to find emotional health for ourselves and how to help others. 9 studies.

Caring for Physical Needs. When we are sick or when our basic needs for food, clothing and adequate housing are not being met, our whole being—body, spirit and emotion—is affected. When we care for the physical needs of others, we are showing God's love. These Bible studies will help you learn to do that. 8 studies.

Caring for People in Conflict. Divided churches. Broken friendships. Angry children. Torn marriages. We all have to deal with conflict and the emotions which accompany it. These studies will show you how God can bring healing and reconciliation. 9 studies.

Caring for People in Grief. Because sin brought death into the world, we all have to look into death's ugly face at one time or another. These Bible studies cover the issues which consume those who are grieving—fear, peace, grace and hope—and show you how to provide them with comfort. 9 studies.